FOREVER CHANGED

STORIES FROM THE
SECOND WORLD WAR

Tim Cook   Britt Braaten

CANADIAN WAR MUSEUM
MUSÉE CANADIEN DE LA GUERRE

Library and Archives Canada
Cataloguing in Publication

Title: Forever changed : stories from the Second World War / Tim Cook and Britt Braaten.

Names: Cook, Tim, 1971- author. | Braaten, Britt, author. Canadian War Museum, issuing body.

Series: Souvenir catalogue series; 26.

Description: Series statement:
Souvenir Catalogue series, ISSN 2291-6385; 26
Catalogue of an exhibition held at the Canadian War Museum, Ottawa, Ontario.
Issued also in French under title: Vies transformées : récits de la Seconde Guerre mondiale.

Identifiers: Canadiana 20200215825
ISBN 9780660252582 (softcover)

Subjects: LCSH: Canadian War Museum—Catalogs.
LCSH: World War, 1939-1945—Personal narratives, Canadian.
LCSH: World War, 1939-1945—Canada.
LCGFT: Catalogs.

Classification: LCC D768.15 .C66 2020
DDC 940.53/71—dc23

Published by the
Canadian War Museum
1 Vimy Place
Ottawa, ON K1A 0M8
warmuseum.ca

Printed and bound in Canada

This work is a souvenir of an exhibition developed by the Canadian War Museum.

Graphic design and cover:
InnovaCom Marketing & Communication

04 – **Foreword**

06 – **Introduction**

12 – **The War at Home**

26 – **The Battle of the Atlantic**

38 – **Canadians in Sicily and Italy**

54 – **Canadians in Northwest Europe**

70 – **The End of the War in Europe**

86 – **The War Against Japan**

108 – **A Country Shaped by War**

117 – **Contributions**

Foreword

The Second World War was a conflict of almost unimaginable scope, dispatching hundreds of millions of people in uniform across the globe and claiming the lives of millions of combatants and civilians. This war was intensely personal and life-changing for those who experienced it.

For Canadians, the war effort was all-consuming. Almost 1.1 million Canadian men and women served in the military at that time, which was significant for a country with a population of only 11.5 million. On the home front,

everyone was affected by the war, be they workers in war-related industries, or family members with loved ones serving abroad.

This souvenir catalogue, which accompanies the Canadian War Museum's exhibition **Forever Changed – Stories From the Second World War**, presents this crucial chapter in world history. Through compelling artifacts and poignant individual stories, it explores the human side of a war whose costs were borne by ordinary people from communities across Canada.

Forever Changed introduces us to Edith Vollrath, who worked as a "munitions girl" in an Ajax, Ontario factory. We also meet Able Seaman George Boyer, a descendant of Louis Riel and part of the crew that guided a damaged warship back to port after a U-boat attack, as well as Major Alex Campbell, who led his soldiers from the front and died in battle in Italy.

The tragedy of war also cast a long and enduring shadow. Nursing Sister Winnie Burwash witnessed devastation in Europe and was deeply affected by the trauma.

On the home front, Albert Socqué was left with serious burns after saving a co-worker from a fire at a munitions factory in Valleyfield, Quebec.

As Canadians commemorate the 75th anniversary of the Second World War, *Forever Changed* provides a human face for a defining event in Canadian and world history.

Caroline Dromaguet
ACTING DIRECTOR GENERAL
Canadian War Museum

Introduction

The Second World War was fought across almost every continent, on land, at sea and in the air. It involved hundreds of millions of people in uniform, serving both on their home territories and abroad.

For most of the countries at war, it was a struggle for survival, during which any weapon or tactic was employed to win or endure. Civilians were killed in the millions as armies rampaged their way through cities, towns, villages and the countryside that lay between. It was a war of bullets, shells and bombers, but also of starvation, terror and genocide.

Following Germany's invasion of Poland on September 1, 1939, Canada declared war. Canadians soon began enlisting in the armed forces to defend Canada and aid Britain. Prime Minister William Lyon Mackenzie King hoped for a war with limited engagement — a war in which Canada would stand by its allies, while not tearing apart fragile national unity along existing or potential new fault lines through an all-out war effort.

But a majority of Canadians wanted more than Mackenzie King's limited war. Eventually, almost 1.1 million men and women would serve in uniform, out of a population of only 11.5 million. Almost everyone else in Canada was also affected by the war — fearful for loved ones in uniform, working in wartime industries and contributing to victory.

Siblings Gwen Jones and Leading Seaman Keith Jones, 1943.

8

This photograph was labelled "Ladies Gossip Circle" by Japanese Canadian teenager Michiko (Ishii) Ayukawa. It depicts Michiko's neighbours, following their forced relocation to Lemon Creek, British Columbia.

Canada's greatest defence against the horrors unleashed in Europe by the Germans and in the Far East by the Japanese, was its geographical position. Despite attacks on the east and west coasts, and along the St. Lawrence River, Canadians on the home front were free to contribute significantly to the war effort without fear of their communities being bombed into ruins. At the same time, although Canada was relatively safe from attack, many Canadians had family members who were suffering under occupation in Europe or Asia.

One of Canada's most significant contributions to the Allied war effort was its agreement, in December 1939, to help implement the British Commonwealth Air Training Plan. The Plan expanded quickly to become a nationwide network of air bases and schools that ultimately trained 131,500 aircrew.

The war changed when Germany overran Western Europe in May 1940. It changed again when Germany invaded the Soviet Union in June 1941, turning Stalin into an improbable ally of the West.

Surprise Japanese attacks are best remembered for an airstrike on Pearl Harbor on December 7, 1941, but throughout the Pacific and Far East, American, British, Filipino and Dutch possessions were under assault.

Two Canadian battalions took part in the defence of Hong Kong. Following a final defeat by the Japanese, soldiers and civilians alike suffered tremendous privation in prisoner-of-war camps. Thousands of other Canadians served in the Far East, primarily in Burma (present-day Myanmar).

Around the world, Canadians in and out of uniform mobilized for a long war. They fought the Germans on the North Atlantic, in the English Channel, in the skies above Europe, in Italy, and in massive land campaigns across Northwest Europe from June 1944 to May 1945.

The cost of victory was high, borne by men and women in uniform, and by their families and communities. Some 45,000 Canadians were killed, and around 55,000 more returned home with physical injuries. Countless others carried invisible scars.

Never, however, had Canada fought a war for more important ideals.

——

Canadian gunners in Sicily, 1943.

The War at Home

Canadians protected supply lines to Europe and supported the Allied war effort. Isolated from German forces in Europe and the Japanese in the Pacific, during the war's early years, Canada contributed military units to defend Britain, while also building up defences along its own east and west coasts.

Industrial production was among Canada's most important contributions to an Allied victory. Canadian workers played a key role in the Allied war effort through massive and varied wartime industries. The output was astonishing: 8,655 ships and small vessels, 42,966 artillery pieces, 800,000 military vehicles, and more than 1.7 million small arms.

From 1939 to 1945, Canada produced $11 billion worth of wartime equipment and food, equivalent to more than $125 billion today.

———

01

Workers assemble tanks at Montreal Locomotive Works in Montréal, Quebec, summer 1943.

Civilians in Wartime

The war touched the lives of civilians in Canada. They worried about loved ones in service, family members trapped in enemy-occupied territory, and the possibility of an attack on Canadian soil. They also mourned their losses.

In other parts of the world, civilians adapted to the realities of war. Londoner Alice Birch created this quilt, stitch by stich, as bombs fell around her. The repetitive activity calmed her nerves whenever she was forced to take refuge in bomb shelters.

Alice's descendants brought the quilt with them when they emigrated to Canada after the war.

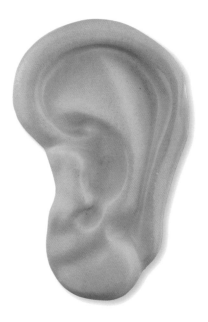

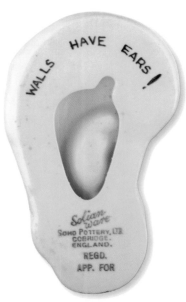

"Walls Have Ears!"

This strange ceramic ornament was a reminder of a real threat. The ear was attached to a wall, warning passersby not to discuss military secrets, as they never knew when the enemy might be listening.

Danger on the Home Front

Albert Socqué, G.M. (1909–1989)

When a load of cellulose nitrate — used in making military explosives — ignited at the rear of his truck, driver Albert Socqué acted fast. He raced into the six-metre-high flames to drag out a co-worker caught in the chemical fire.

Although Albert's rescue effort left him with serious burns, both men survived. For his heroism and self-sacrifice, Albert received the George Medal, one of the highest recognitions for bravery. Albert was only one of three Canadians to receive the medal during the Second World War.

The George Medal was instituted in 1940 by King George VI, during the German bombing campaign known as the Blitz. It recognizes acts of civilian courage.

A Wartime Worker

Edith (Vollrath) Whitford (1925–)

Checking airplane engines for cracks and pouring liquid explosives into bomb casings may seem like unusual work for a teenager — but not in wartime Canada.

In early 1944, at the age of 18, Edith Vollrath started working with Aircraft Repair Limited in Edmonton, Alberta. Nearly a year later, she was transferred to Defence Industries Limited in Ajax, Ontario. Edith was one of 300,000 Canadian women who held wartime-production jobs during the Second World War.

After the war, Edith returned home to Alberta, married, and raised seven children.

■ ■

Edith Vollrath on break at Defence Industries Limited, Ajax, Ontario, 1945.

The number of women working outside the home doubled during the war, from 600,000 to 1.2 million. This sculpture captures the likeness of one wartime worker — a "munitions girl" like Edith.

While working at Defence Industries Limited, in Ajax, Ontario, Edith handled dangerous materials used in the production of artillery shells. She was hospitalized after explosive powder burned her face, but soon recovered and returned to work.

The Munitions Girl

Carved by August Porter Abolit
between 1939 and 1945
Wood

Defence Industries Limited shell filling department.

Training aircrew under the British Commonwealth Air Training Plan was one of Canada's major contributions to the Allied war effort. An astonishing 131,500 aircrew attended schools across Canada. Edith did her part to keep trainee aircrews safe by checking planes for damage.

Canada also built aircraft. Some 104,000 men and women worked in the aircraft industry across Canada. They produced more than 16,000 planes for Canadian and other Allied air forces.

Maintenance Jobs in the Hangar

Painted by Paraskeva Clark in 1945
Oil on canvas

Training Aircrew in Canada

Flight Lieutenant George Albert Reynolds (1917–2005)

Located far from enemy attack, and offering vast open spaces, Canada was an ideal air-training ground. Instructors like George Reynolds made this possible.

George showed an aptitude for teaching, even while a student himself. In near-daily letters to his fiancée, Helen Grant, he included calculations and diagrams to help her understand his coursework. After graduating at the top of his class, George spent the war training others.

———

Flight Lieutenant George Reynolds, around 1943.

The Battle of the Atlantic

The Battle of the Atlantic ran from the first day of the war to the last, making it the longest continuous campaign of the Second World War.

The Royal Canadian Navy was tasked with protecting vulnerable civilian merchant vessels. Operated by Merchant Navy personnel, the ships were frequently targeted by German U-boats (submarines), which sought to sever the lifeline of war supplies from North America.

The use of convoys for protection, the development of new tactics and radar technology, as well as additional air support, inflicted serious losses on the U-boats by May 1943. Most retreated to Europe, but they continued to attack merchant vessels and warships. The cost in lives remained high until the end of the war.

02

**Convoy Under Attack –
North Atlantic**

Painted by Tom Wood between 1939 and 1945
Oil on canvas

Rough Seas

This battered flag evokes the rough seas of the North Atlantic. It was flown from HMCS *Arrowhead*, a Canadian corvette that protected merchant vessels crossing the ocean.

Stories at Sea

Able Seaman George William Boyer (1922–1979)

Even far from his Saskatchewan home, George Boyer kept his family close. The seaman, who could trace his ancestry to Métis leader Louis Riel, spent his leisure time writing letters to his mother and his 12 older siblings.

George served on several ships involved in protecting merchant vessels against German U-boat attack in the Atlantic.

This was the primary role of the Royal Canadian Navy. There could be no invasion of Europe — or extended campaigns in other theatres of war — without military supplies from North America.

▬ ▬

Able Seaman George Boyer during the Second World War.

In the summer of 1944, George was serving on HMS *Nabob*, a Ruler-class escort aircraft carrier crewed by Canadians. The ship was part of an operation to sink the feared German battleship *Tirpitz*, stationed off the coast of enemy-occupied Norway.

On August 22, 1944, at 5:16 p.m., *Nabob* was preparing to fuel an escort vessel when German submarine *U-354* struck. A torpedo tore a 10-metre hole in the steel hull.

George was part of a skeleton crew that guided the badly damaged *Nabob* to Scapa Flow, Scotland. The five-day journey was fraught with danger.

▬ ▬

Medal Set, Able Seaman George William Boyer

1. 1939-1945 Star
2. Atlantic Star
3. Canadian Volunteer Service
4. War Medal 1939-1945

1.   2.   3.   4.

31

Twenty-one sailors were killed in the torpedoing of HMS *Nabob* on August 22, 1944, including Able Seaman David "Dave" Melrose, a close friend of George.

George wrote to his mother of the loss:

"I lost Dave my pal. . . . [W]e were just like brothers, Dave and I. So you can see how damned hard it was when he left us. That's the way it is, one minute talking to him the next minute he's gone."

Mindful of censorship, George left his letter deliberately vague, with no details of how Dave died. The attack on *Nabob* would not be reported in Canadian newspapers until July 1945.

Letter from George Boyer to
his mother, Mary Rosalie Boyer,
September 8, 1944.

Sept. 8

Dear Mom,

It's been ages since I've written to you. I hope this letter reaches you okay and soon. I meant to send you a cablegram but I haven't been up town for months, so wasn't able to.

I am very well. As you notice I have a change of address, which means to say I expect to be sent home soon. I am in a sort of transit camp at the present time. Now don't go getting ideas as I am in perfect health, nothing the matter with me at all.

I lost Dave my pal. I guess you understand what I mean, that's the way it goes, some of us I suppose some of us were just luckier than the others. Dave was a grand guy, perhaps I have written about him before, but ever since we were brothers Dave and I. So you can see how damned hard it was when he left us. That's the way it is, one minute talking to him the next minute he's gone. I can't tell you any more on account of censorship, but I guess you can understand.

It's all very quiet out here and very comfortable. They treat us okay. I hope it lasts for some time until we leave this and anyway shouldn't be too long.

Don't say goodnights, please don't worry as all activity is over for me for a while. I hope to be seeing you soon so. Cheerio! Keep your chin up. Goodnight Mom.

My love.
George.

A Teenage Sailor

Leading Seaman Keith Edward Jones
(1924–2018)

On his first Atlantic crossing, 17-year-old sailor Keith Jones was part of a convoy that lost 17 ships to German U-boats. For Keith, the dangers would only continue.

His warship was part of the action on D-Day, June 6, 1944, supporting the Allied invasion of Normandy. His diary entry for that day reads "We can't see the land for fire and smoke. It sounds like thunder. . . . German bomber just made an attack no hits."

—

Leading Seaman Keith Jones on ship during the Second World War.

4 to day is sunday blacklistmen don't have to work 3 padres aboard

5 landing barges on the move we sliped at 17.00 to take up position at head hundreds of planes all over 23.00 action stations can see tom's landing on French coast + fires

6 07.45 the big ships have been shelling we cant see land for fire + smoke it sounds like thunder 1925 German bombers just made an attack no hits para troops going in the sky is full of bombers + fighters four lancasters + shot down 13.30 big fires along coast two destroyers sunk 23.00 Germans attacked no loss

8 troop ships coming in all night HMS RODNY bombarding we cant see horizon for ships German bomber shot down the sky is red with A-A fire + exploding bombs 09.3E sunk

9 hospital ships + floating forts + troops came in fired at four ME.109 but they turned away in time HMS RAMILLIES fired to 1 plane + 1 E boat sunk cruisers are still bombarding long range

10 cruisers are still bombarding hundreds of troop ships are coming in we joined our flotila + patrolled Le Hirer + River Siene for German destroyers they never came out

11 troop ships still coming in Rodny + Nelson bombarding cana diens driven back but are still farthest in we joined the 600 + patrolled Le Hirer + River Sien

12 6 minesweepers came out this morning we are laying smoke screen + protecting them 1330 enemy guns firing at us we straddled one man hit with shrapnel 0400 five bombers just missed us shaded not a light no orders to open fire did anyway

13 portable dock coming in troops + tanks coming in a small airfield has been built out on patrole by ourselves bait for E boats cruisers standing by 0600 nothing happened

Husband and Wife

Robert "Bob" Bush (1919–2003)
Evangeline (Harrold) Bush (1919–1999)

As a member of the British Merchant Navy (1936–1941) and the Canadian Merchant Navy (1941–1945), Bob Bush faced more than his share of danger. At various points, his ships were torpedoed, bombed, machine-gunned and shelled.

Evangeline Harrold's time in the Women's Royal Canadian Naval Service was less dangerous, although still eventful. Posted to a plotting room in Halifax, Nova Scotia, she processed intelligence reports, and tracked the movements of Allied vessels and German submarines.

Evangeline and Bob met in Halifax and married soon after.

___

Service Dress Caps, Robert Bush and Evangeline Harrold

Evangeline (Harrold) Bush
and Bob Bush, between
1944 and 1945.

Canadians in Sicily and Italy

Canadian naval, air and ground forces played a significant role in battles against Italian and German troops in Sicily and mainland Italy.

After the May 1943 defeat of Axis forces in North Africa, the Allies pushed north across the Mediterranean, invading Sicily on July 10, 1943, and the Italian mainland on September 3, 1943.

With the first Canadian land campaign of the war in Sicily and Italy, the Canadians earned a reputation as effective soldiers, winning a series of important victories against a determined enemy.

—

03

Private M. D. White of The Loyal Edmonton Regiment, observing from a defensive position, Colle d'Anchise, Italy, October 26, 1943.

A Combat Leader

Major Alexander "Alex" Railton Campbell (1910–1943)

For Alex Campbell, the war against Germany was undeniably personal. His father was killed in the First World War, and Alex saw this new conflict as an opportunity to make his family proud and avenge his father.

As an officer in The Hastings and Prince Edward Regiment, Alex was an inspiration to the men he led, as well as to his fellow officers. One described him as "not only a magnificent fighter, but a deep thinker as well."

— —

Major Alex Campbell, 1940.

BLACK & OTHERS, LTD.
MONTREAL, CANADA

Somewhere in England
Aug 4th.

the train   en and every
                            friends. It
                              to bring

Dear Mother.

received m
now and
arrived

trip over
the best
everyth
us com
could
you
trip

200
qui
an
fu

Tomorrow I have to get the rest of my equipment. Revolver & belts etc. I took quite a few pictures before I left. and I will send some to you later on.

Lots of love mother dear and don't worry about ~~not~~ me. My biggest worry is that I may not be as good a soldier as I should be to live up to Daddy. but I will do my best and with your prayers I should succeed.

xxxxxxx Love and Kisses
xxxxxxx
xxxxxx

Alex

When Alex enlisted, he felt the pressure of following in his soldier father's footsteps. He admitted to his mother, "My biggest worry is that I may not be as good a soldier as I should be to live up to Daddy."

Alex rose to the occasion. Like his father before him, Alex was mentioned in despatches in recognition of his extraordinary service.

▬ ▬

Letter from Alex Campbell to his mother, Sarah Jane Campbell, August 3, 1940.

At the Battle of Valguarnera, in Sicily, on July 18, 1943, Alex led an attack on a German convoy of trucks. One of the men under his command that day was Farley Mowat, who would go on to make his name as an author.

Mowat later recalled that "the rattle and roar of small arms and grenades rose to a crescendo . . . and the stretch of road below us became a slaughterhouse."

About 90 Germans were killed. Alex, in his own words, "accounted for 18."

Medal Set, Major Alexander Railton Campbell

1. 1939-1945 Star
2. Africa Star with North Africa 1942-1943 Bar
3. Italy Star
4. Defence Medal
5. Canadian Volunteer Service Medal with Overseas Bar
6. War Medal 1939-1945 with Oak Leaf

1.   2.

3.   4.   5.   6.

Alex had a reputation for toughness.
While serving in Sicily in August 1943,
he was shot in the arm. A few weeks later,
in Italy, he was shot again — this time in
the head. Neither wound stopped him.

His death in battle on December 25, 1943,
shocked everyone who knew him. Even
the best soldiers were not invulnerable.

Before his final battle, Alex wrote this
poignant poem on the stress and strain
of leadership.

A Prayer Before Battle

When 'neath the rumble of the guns,
I lead my men against the Huns,
'Tis then I feel so all alone and weak and scared,
And oft I wonder how I dared,
Accept the task of leading men.

I wonder, worry, fret, and then I pray,
Oh God! Who promised oft
To humble men a listening ear,
Now in my spirit's troubled state,
Draw near, dear God, draw near, draw near.

Make me more willing to obey,
Help me to merit my command,
And if this be my fatal day,
Reach out, Oh God, Thy Guiding Hand,
And lead me down that deep, dark vale.

These men of mine must never know
How much afraid I really am,
Help me to lead them in the fight
So they will say, "He was a man."

— Alex Campbell, 1943

Wedding of Trooper Gordon
Fennell and Joyce Fennell,
May 15, 1945.

Life-Saving Shoes

Trooper Gordon Fennell (1922–)

Gordon Fennell's mother sent dress shoes from Canada for his wedding to his British fiancée, Joyce. Gordon stored the shoes in his tank for safekeeping.

On October 4, 1943, Gordon's tank was blown up in Italy. He escaped with minor injuries, thanks in part to the shoes, which caught some of the shrapnel that might otherwise have ended his life.

When Gordon and Joyce married in May 1945, he did not wear the battle-damaged shoes. But he kept them for more than 70 years.

Breaching the Hitler Line

In Italy, on May 24, 1944, the Allies broke through the central German defensive position known as the Hitler Line. Canadian artist Charles Comfort saw the devastation of the battle firsthand, as he depicted the Canadians fighting their way forward.

——

The Hitler Line

Painted by Charles Comfort in 1944
Oil on canvas

Serving With Distinction

Lieutenant-Colonel John Keefer Mahony, V.C., C.D. (1911–1990)

For his actions on May 24, 1944, John Mahony was awarded the Victoria Cross, the Commonwealth's highest award for bravery in battle.

Tasked with establishing a vital bridgehead over the Melfa River in Italy, his company of The Westminster Regiment held their ground for five hours, in the face of relentless enemy attack.

Mahony's Victoria Cross citation notes that he served "with absolute fearlessness and disregard for his own safety."

Medal Set, Lieutenant-Colonel
John Keefer Mahony, V.C., C.D.

1. Victoria Cross
2. 1939-1945 Star
3. Italy Star
4. Defence Medal
5. Canadian Volunteer Service Medal and Bar
6. War Medal 1939-1945
7. Queen Elizabeth II Coronation Medal 1953
8. Canadian Centennial Medal 1967
9. Queen Elizabeth II Silver Jubilee Medal 1977
10. Canadian Efficiency Medal
11. Canadian Forces Decoration

1.   2.   3.   4.   5.   6.   7.   8.   9.   10.   11.

Canadians in Northwest Europe

High above the battlefield, squadrons of Canadian fighters and bombers wreaked havoc on the enemy. At sea, the Royal Canadian Navy, Royal Canadian Air Force, and the Merchant Navy served together to transport crucial supplies across the Atlantic. In Italy, almost 100,000 Canadians fought their way northward.

At the same time, all eyes were on the Canadian army in Northwest Europe, as they ground forward during the 11 months following D-Day in a series of difficult battles against German forces in France, Belgium, the Netherlands and Germany.

Victory was eventually achieved, but at a terrible price.

04

A Reminder of Home

While serving in Europe, Wing Commander Malcolm Ferguson of 419 Squadron, Royal Canadian Air Force, had the nose of his Lancaster Mark X bomber decorated with a portrait of his young daughter, Christine.

Known as nose art, this kind of artistic personalization further bonded airmen to their aircraft.

—

The Liberation of Northwest Europe

After years of planning, the Allies invaded Normandy, France, on June 6, 1944. It would be a key turning point in the war.

German defences were heavily fortified. Allied planners had reason to fear that the invading force would be annihilated on the beaches.

This would prove not to be the case. With the support of thousands of aircraft and warships, the Allies clawed their way ashore.

Over the next 11 weeks, the Allied forces, including the Canadians, defeated the Germans in battle, liberating Normandy.

The Mk III helmet was issued to British and Canadian soldiers for D-Day. It became a symbol of the day, representing the toughness of those who were there.

Laying the Groundwork

Major Gustave Daniel Alfred "Guy" Biéler, D.S.O., M.B.E. (1904–1944)

Having lived in France until the age of 20, Montréal resident Major Guy Biéler was familiar with French culture, language and geography. He put that knowledge to use during the war. For 15 months, Guy acted as a Special Operations Executive (SOE) agent in France.

Guy organized sabotage missions and served as a liaison between the French Resistance and the Allies, preparing for the Allied invasion of France. He was captured in January 1944, and executed by firing squad in September of that year.

After his death, a senior SOE officer remarked that "[Guy] and the brave men who worked with him truly paved the way for the successful landing in June 1944."

Guy Biéler with one of his children in Montréal before the war.

Guy Biéler's false identification
card, used in the field.

June 4 1944

Dear parents, brothers & sisters

My time for writing is very limited. However I must write a few words just to let you know how things are going.

First of all, thanks a million for the cigs & parcels and letters. Received your letter, Dad, just a day ago. By mistake I received Len's cigs. too.

Sorry Mom that I don't have time to answer all your questions now.

Dad, the time has come for that long awaited day, the invasion of France. Yes, I am in. I'll be in the first hundred Canadians to land by parachute. I know our job well. We have been training for all conditions & circumstances. We have a fair chance. I am not certain but I expect Len will be coming a few days later.

To go in as a Paratrooper was entirely my own choice. I am in no way connected with a

A D-Day Parachutist

Private Leslie Abram Neufeld (1922–1944)

Leslie Neufeld was torn between his pacifist Mennonite upbringing and a desire to serve his country. He initially joined the Royal Canadian Army Medical Corps, but later volunteered as a parachutist, looking to fight the Germans in the coming invasion of Europe.

Leslie wrote a letter to his family the day before he was dropped into Normandy. "This job is dangerous, very dangerous," he penned. "If anything should happen to me, do not feel sad or burdened by it."

Leslie was one of the 359 Canadian army servicemen killed on D-Day.

Letter from Leslie Neufeld to parents Henry and Anna and siblings Richard, Leonard, Leonora, Arthur, Edward, Elvina, Verna and Donelda, June 4, 1944.

A Mother Mourns

Alta R. Wilkinson (1898–1990)

Twenty-four-year-old Private Arthur
Wilkinson was killed in combat on
July 18, 1944, during the Normandy
campaign.

His mother, Alta, was devastated by
the loss. Following Arthur's death, she
collected letters, telegrams, relics and
photographs related to his war service.
In three volumes, she painstakingly built
this documentary tribute to her son.

Private Arthur Wilkinson and his
mother, Alta Wilkinson,
December 7, 1939.

Alta's scrapbooks include the telegram announcing Arthur's death, notes of condolence from the Minister of Defence and King George VI, and a photograph of her son's grave marker.

Documenting the War

Sergeant Hugh McCaughey (1906–1973)

Hugh McCaughey spent two years capturing film footage of the Canadians in Europe.

He followed the army through France, the Netherlands and Germany, filming combat, celebrations and the daily lives of servicemen and servicewomen.

Hugh took great pains to ensure that his footage was clear and compelling. It was never easy to film on the front lines, under the threat of enemy snipers and shelling. Shaky hands, poor light and fragile equipment could result in unusable footage.

Having proven himself on the battlefields of Europe, Hugh had high hopes for a postwar career in the movie industry. Instead, he returned to Vancouver, British Columbia, where he worked as a camera salesman.

Hugh's footage and that of other Canadian combat cameramen has helped shape our understanding of Canada's Second World War experience to this day.

▬ ▬

Sergeant Hugh McCaughey
in the Netherlands,
January 30, 1945.

[Background large handwriting, partially visible:]

) couldnt tell you ab...
in Paris, it would be imp...
the fact that Paris had bee...

[Letterhead on letter pages:]

CANADIAN LEGION
WAR SERVICES Inc.

CANADIAN
KNIGHTS OF COLUMBUS
WAR SERVICES

CANADIAN Y.M.C.A.
OVERSEAS

THE SALVATION ARMY
CANADIAN
WAR SERVICES

ON ACTIVE SERVICE

[Center letter page:]

2.

at the grave of the unknown soldier,
under the Arc-de-Triomphe.

I couldnt tell you about my reception
in Paris, it would be impossible, in spite of
the fact that Paris had been liberated for 10
days when I got there. But there hadn't been
more than fifty Canadians there and the
people went wild when they read my shoulder
patches.

Here's a story by way of illustration... The
scene is the Arc-de-Triomphe. Millions of people
line the streets to see Eisenhower dedicate a
plaque to the liberation of Paris. De Gaulle and
a host of other celebrities are there. Your
brother is a lone Canadian and finds at
least 20 American movie men with their
cameras, motors and expensive
equipment, commanding every place of
advantage. The English photographers are out
in force too, and so "still" men are falling
all over themselves. I elect to shoot long shots
and cut in crowd scenes and such shots
as firemen lining the rooftops with their
guns at the ready. I walk down the
Boulevard Champs Elysees, with my camera

[Bottom fragment, center page:]

was a preview...
of time and I trie...
and that is never a success...
next day I Premier Drew laying a wreath
of ... and ...
CFA 170   PLEASE WRITE ON BOTH SIDES

[Right letter page:]

3 and tripod on my shoulder. Someone
reads my patches and yells "Canadienne".
The crowd takes it up, they shout and
yell and push forward, trying to break
through the line of Gendarmes who are
lining the route. I'm worried that they
will make it and ease out towards the
centre of the boulevard, waving and
acknowledging their shouts of "merci"
and "thank you". To Hell with Eisenhower -
Hughie Mc Caughey from Vancouver is in
town. That will give you an idea of what
it's like to be a celebrity. But unless it
has happened to you, it is hard to believe
that people actually came up to me in the
streets and touched my uniform as if
I was a spiritual healer.

Gosh I can't get the time to write
letters. I just had dinner and now
I'm leaving for Belgium for the
afternoon.

But let's get Paris straight here first,
while I am waiting for a jeep to
pick me up. The first impression of
Paris is the beautiful women - from
the knees up, as they all ride bicycles
and wear flimsy frocks that fly

I made a connection there too
Frenchman came up to me and sa...
front and back and even ta...

CFA 170   PLEASE WRITE ON BOTH SIDES

[Left letter page, partial:]

Dear Don:

Ha...
at the same...
with you re...
time. I'll t...
your i...
bench in t...
yard - cow...
miles from...
But ...
was there...
I made...
no wo...
of the...
breath...
I ...
cover t...
abou...

As the Canadians advanced through Northwest Europe in 1944 and 1945, Hugh was right there with them, recording their actions. He also captured footage of liberated civilians.

Hugh regaled his brother, Don, with a story of filming in recently liberated Paris, France: "Someone reads my patches and yells '*Canadien*.' The crowd takes it up, they shout and yell and push forward, trying to break through the line of Gendarmes who are lining the route. . . . To Hell with Eisenhower, Hughie McCaughey from Vancouver is in town."

Letter from Sergeant Hugh McCaughey
to his brother Don McCaughey,
September 10, 1944.

A Famous Photograph

Private Mary (Greyeyes) Reid (1920–2011)

Canadians worked to distinguish their armed forces from the British and Americans. This involved creating identifiable Canadian units and symbols. These efforts fostered pride in the service and sacrifice of Canadians.

When Mary Greyeyes joined the Canadian Women's Army Corps, she was looking for opportunities beyond those available on the Maskêko-Sâkahikanihk (Muskeg Lake Cree Nation) reserve. She never imagined that her image would be seen around the world.

In June 1942, Mary was asked to appear in a promotional photograph, in exchange for lunch and a new uniform. Harry Ball, an Indigenous First World War veteran, was paid $20 to do the same. Mary knelt before him, the photographer captured the scene, and the image became part of our history.

The photograph appeared in newspapers across Canada and Britain. For decades, it carried the caption: "Unidentified Indian princess getting blessing from her chief and father to go fight in the war."

In fact, "princess" is a European concept that was frequently misapplied to young Indigenous women. Harry was neither a Chief nor her father; and the scene was an imitation ceremony, done for the benefit of the camera.

——

Private Mary Greyeyes,
from Maskêko-Sâkahikanihk
(Muskeg Lake Cree Nation),
Canadian Women's Army Corps,
with Harry Ball, Piapot First Nation.

The End of the War in Europe

Canadian forces in Europe fought almost continuously from the D-Day invasion of June 6, 1944, to victory in Europe on May 8, 1945.

But the tragedy and trauma of the war in Europe did not end with Germany's surrender in May 1945. Wounded service personnel and sick civilians needed to be treated. In addition, hundreds of thousands of Canadian military personnel were to be discharged from service and returned home.

05

Private Jane Shaddock,
Private Martin MacPherson
and Private Polly Pollyblank
entering Hamm, Germany,
June 12, 1945.

"V" for Victory

This flag was given to 16-year-old Richard
Thorman on Victory in Europe Day (VE Day).
Wearing his air cadet uniform, Richard
walked to his school in Scarborough,
Ontario, hoping to celebrate with friends.
No one was there. He had missed the
party, but kept the flag as a memento
of this important day.

—

VE-DAY
MAY 8, 1945

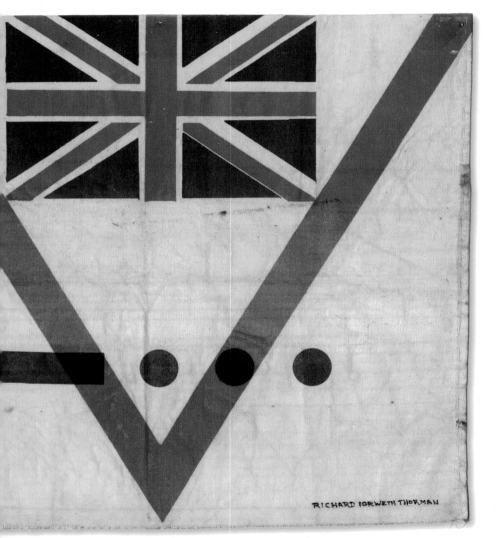

RICHARD IORWETH THORMAN

73

Lieutenant (Nursing Sister) Winnie Burwash during the Second World War.

After the Fighting

Nursing Sister Winnifred "Winnie" Burwash (1910–1987)

"You don't have to be on the front lines to see tragedy," wrote Winnie Burwash to her friends back in Montréal, Quebec, in April 1944. Although stationed at a hospital in southern England, she still treated Canadians sent to Britain to recover from their wounds. She was later posted to the Continent, arriving after VE Day, and worked in hospitals in Germany and the Netherlands.

She returned to Canada on February 2, 1946. While her homecoming was eagerly anticipated, many veterans suffered from physical illnesses and mental health problems. According to her family, Winnie had depression. It is not known whether her wartime service exacerbated her condition. Winnie died by suicide in 1987.

▬ ▬

In June 1945, Winnie arrived in Germany. She saw devastation all around her, as the last remnants of Nazi Germany were dismantled, and reconstruction began.

There, Winnie cared for the desperately ill people who emerged from concentration camps and labour camps, following years of German mistreatment. Their captors had deliberately created conditions in which deadly diseases killed tens of thousands. Corpses lay in massive open graves. Prisoners were sick and starving.

The Canadians who witnessed these horrors were traumatized by what they saw.

Canadian Padre J. Alphonse Marcoux salvaged the head from a demolished statue of German dictator Adolf Hitler, and kept it as a souvenir.

Belsen Concentration Camp — Malnutrition

Drawn by Aba Bayefsky in 1945
Charcoal and Conté crayon on paper

"My life here isn't on the even keel it was in England," wrote Winnie from her posting in the Netherlands, "what with working and parties and trying to get enough sleep."

While she worked hard to care for patients, her letters included frequent accounts of parties, drinking and men. Winnie was not alone in enjoying certain aspects of the overseas wartime experience. Many service personnel and civilians reacted to the difficulties of war by making the most of what enjoyment they could find. War was dangerous and stressful, but it also brought new freedoms.

———

Private Virginia Stansell Singing, Tivoli Theatre, Apeldoorn, C Unit Canadian Army Shows

Painted by Molly Lamb Bobak in 1945
Watercolour, ink and graphite on paper

Putting on a Show

Private Minnie Eleanor Gray (1912–2005)

Minnie Gray considered her years in
the Canadian Women's Army Corps to
be the highlight of her life. From July 1945
to February 1946, she served as chaperone
to an all-female military pipe band stationed
in Apeldoorn, the Netherlands.

She accompanied the band as they
entertained troops and civilians, making
lifelong friends along the way.

Private Minnie Gray during
the Second World War.

The CWAC Pipe Band performing at
the Arc de Triomphe in Paris, France,
November 4, 1945.

Welcome Home

Private Milton Henry DeMeuleneare (1923–2013)

The return to civilian life after years in the military could be daunting. The Government of Canada launched programs, known collectively as the Veterans Charter, which offered a range of benefits to returning servicemen and servicewomen.

Milton DeMeuleneare served with the Royal Canadian Electrical and Mechanical Engineers, keeping vehicles running. When the war ended, he returned to Canada and resumed his trade as a tool and die maker.

—

Private Milton DeMeuleneare with his mother, Margaret, upon his return from Europe, with a "Welcome Home Son" sign on display in the window, 1946.

Returning to Civvy Street

Before discharge, all military personnel were given complete medical and dental examinations to identify any conditions in need of further treatment. Posters like this provided details about medical, educational and financial provisions for veterans.

Note: *Periods of absence without leave, or leave w*
pay, do not count as service for any grant or U

MEDICAL EXAMINATION

To see if you are as fit to do a job as when you joined up, or if not,

   (a) what treatment you need

   (b) what pension you may qualify for

DENTAL EXAMINATION

You are entitled to treatment after you leave the Service, if:

   (a) this exam shows you need it

   (b) you apply within 90 days of discharge

DISCHARGE PAPERS

These will normally be given you, after you see the Counsellor at the Depot nearest either:

   (a) the place where you enlisted

   or (b) the place where you intend to live

CLOTHING ALLOWANCE—$100

For those discharged after July 31, 1944.

REHABILITATION GRANT

If you have served 183 days or more, you are entitled to one month's pay of your rank, plus one month's dependents' allowances, as of the time of discharge.

TRANSPORTATION

You will receive a railway warrant to your place of enlistment; or elsewhere, if cost is not greater.

WAR SERVICE GRATUITY

This is applied for on discharge:

BASIC GRATUITY	**PLUS**	SUPPLEMENTARY GRATUITY
$7.50 per month of Volunteer Service in Western Hemisphere.		7 days' pay and allowances (as at date of discharge) for each 6 months' Service overseas or in the Aleutians.
$15 per month for Service overseas or in the Aleutians.		

TOTAL is paid to you in monthly instalments no one of which is greater than your monthly pay and dependents' and subsistence allowances while you're in the Service.

But you must apply

TRAINING PROVISIONS

You are eligible for needed training for civilian life. While training you will be given :

(a) Your fees. (b) Living allowance up to $60 per month for a single man, up to $90 for a man and wife, plus allowance for dependents.

You Can Apply For :

VOCATIONAL TRAINING

Your training will not normally be paid for longer than 12 months (or the length of time you served if less). If you served more than a year your training can be extended if necessary. Many will be trained on the job with wages, if necessary supplemented by a government allowance.

UNIVERSITY EDUCATION

If you qualify for entrance to University within 15 months of discharge, you may receive payments for the time you served as long as your studies are satisfactory. Outstanding students may have allowances extended.

VETERANS' LAND ACT

The Administration can help you to finance land, buildings, stock and equipment worth up to $6000.

The maximum amount for live stock and farm equipment is $1200. You pay: (a) a down payment of 10% of cost of land and buildings; plus (b) two-thirds of cost of land and buildings in instalments which may last up to 25 years. Interest is at 3½%. If you keep up your instalments for 10 years you get: (a) nearly ¼ the value of the land and buildings, free; maximum: $1120, plus (b) value of stock and equipment, free; maximum: $1200.

No Time Limit

FARMS

Practical farming experience is required. You may take training to gain experience or brush up, but people with a city background are not encouraged in full time farming.

SMALL HOLDING

For the man with a regular job or income: farming experience not essential. Land in low-tax areas for spare-time gardening, light stock raising, etc.

FISHING

Experience in commercial fishing required. Equipment allowance may be used for gear, and two veterans may pool equipment allowances.

ALSO / OR / AND

THIS / OR / THIS

if applicable

RE-ESTABLISHMENT CREDIT

(you must apply, showing how you would use the credit due to you.)

IF you don't want Vocational or University training, or benefits under the Veterans' Land Act; or if the value of what you do want under one of those headings is less than the amount of your RE-ESTABLISHMENT CREDIT, (which equals your Basic War Service Gratuity), you may use that Credit, or the remainder of it, to:

BUY, BUILD, REPAIR OR MODERNIZE YOUR HOUSE

You may use the Credit due to you:
(a) to make up to two-thirds of the down payment
(b) to reduce your present mortgage
(c) repair or modernize the house you're going to live in

BUY FURNITURE OR HOUSEHOLD EQUIPMENT

You may use the Credit due to you to pay up two-thirds of the cost of household equipment for domestic use.

PAY INSURANCE PREMIUMS

You may use the Credit due to you to pay premiums on Insurance issued by the Canadian Government.

BUY A BUSINESS

You may use the Credit due to you to make up to two-thirds of the down payment on a Business or Practice which you are qualified to run.

BUY INSTRUMENTS, TOOLS, EQUIPMENT

You may use the Credit due to you to purchase tools, instruments, or equipment necessary for your calling.

PROVIDE WORKING CAPITAL

You may use the Credit due to you as a source of Working Capital for your business or profession.

YOUR OLD JOB

If you had a job for three months, which you left to join up, and the employment still exists, your employer has to take you back on as good terms as if you had never left—provided you apply within a specified time.

CIVIL SERVICE JOBS

Any veteran with a pensionable disability, or any veteran who has served overseas, if he qualifies, is given a preference over civilians or over those who have had service in Canada only, in the selection of Civil Servants.

AWAITING-RETURNS GRANTS

If you start a business or a farm, and have to wait some time for it to pay returns, you may be eligible for a living allowance of up to $50 a month for a single man, $70 for a man and wife, plus an allowance for dependents.

UNEMPLOYMENT INSURANCE

If you get a job covered by Unemployment Insurance, and stay there for 15 weeks, you get insurance credit for all the time you spent in the Service after June 30, 1941, the date when the Act came into force.

VETERANS' INSURANCE

Any time up to three years after discharge, except in a few cases, you may take out a government life policy up to $10,000, without having a medical examination. This is a good way to insure the future of your family.

you may need

HEALTH BENEFITS

Allowances to see you through Temporary Illness, necessary Hospitalization, or Out-patient Treatments, will be paid under certain circumstances. See your Rehabilitation Officer or Veterans' Affairs Representative for the details.

PENSIONS

Permanent disabilities suffered overseas or on duty in Canada, but not resulting from your misconduct, will qualify you for a pension, according to the degree of disability. Pensioners may also get special Treatment Benefits.

OUT-OF-WORK BENEFIT

Any time in the first 18 months after your discharge, IF you are fit for work, but work can't be found, you may draw a living allowance of $50 a month for a single man, $70 for a man and wife, plus allowance for dependents. This can be paid for 12 months, (or the length of time you served, if less).

Prepared by the Wartime Information Board and the National Film Board, for the Inter-Departmental Committee on Rehabilitation Information.   Issued by the Government of Canada.

The War Against Japan

Canadians took part in the struggle to free Southeast Asia from Japanese occupation. Although Canada's primary focus was the war against Germany, Canadian military forces also fought in the Pacific.

On December 8, 1941, the Japanese invaded the British colony of Hong Kong. Canadians were caught in the conflict. Two Canadian battalions, along with supporting troops and nursing sisters, had been sent to strengthen the British garrison at Hong Kong in late 1941. After heroic and costly fighting, the doomed garrison surrendered on December 25, 1941.

Of the 2,000 Canadians serving in Hong Kong, 290 were killed and 483 wounded. The battle continued for the survivors, who endured terrible conditions in Japanese prison camps.

—

06

Canadian soldiers training on Hong Kong Island prior to the Japanese invasion in December 1941.

Love and Luck

Japanese servicemen carried *yosegaki Hinomaru* (good-luck flags), inscribed with messages of victory and safety from loved ones.

This flag is adorned with more than 150 different names and sayings, including "praying for lasting fortune in warfare," "heroism and service" and "the power of 1,000 people."

祝 臼井博君

祝 臼井博君

武運長久

The Prisoner of War Experience

Signalman William Allister (1920–2008)

When William Allister learned that he was shipping out in late 1941, he hoped he was bound for Britain. Instead, he was sent to Hong Kong.

Within weeks of his arrival, the Japanese attacked. William was captured and spent the rest of the war as a prisoner. To cope with the strain, William painted. He used improvised art supplies: crankshaft oil and stolen pieces of tent took the place of oil paints and artist canvas.

Untitled

Painted by William Allister in 1942
Oil on canvas

Poseh Detachment,
British Army Aid Group, CHINA.

No.:   PS/P/20

Name: William Chong Gun

Age: 30

Occupation: Interpreter

Date of
Employment: 1st May 1942

Signature of
Officer-in-Charge:

..................Lt.Col.,
O.C., Poseh Dett., B.A.A.G.

Date issued: 13th July 1945

Date expired: 31st Dec. 1945

英軍服務團百色辦事處

華

聯

姓名 鄺根

年齡 三十

籍貫 廣東台山

貼相片處

職別 翻譯

號數 百字第貳拾號

發給日期 民卅四年七月十三

作廢日期 民卅四年十二月卅一日

主管簽名 梅攬意中校

Behind Enemy Lines

William "Bill" Gun Chong, B.E.M. (1911–2006)

Born and raised in Vancouver, British Columbia, Bill Chong was in Hong Kong, handling his father's estate, when the Japanese invaded. Fearing for his life, he fled to China, where he was recruited by the Allies as an undercover agent. He was known as "Agent 50."

Bill risked his life travelling through Japanese-occupied territories under the auspices of the British Army Aid Group. He smuggled medical supplies in, and guided stranded aviators out.

———

Civilian Prisoners

Frederick Charles "Reg" Oppen (1906–2007)
Hermena Jean Oppen (1911–2005)

When Hong Kong fell to the Japanese, newlyweds Reg and Jean Oppen were interned together. For more than 19 months, they endured deprivation and indignity, until they were released in a prisoner exchange in September 1943. They brought only their Japanese army blankets, stitched with their name. Their few remaining possessions were given to internees who remained behind.

Wedding of Reg Oppen and
Jean Oppen in Hong Kong,
August 31, 1940.

A Promising Pilot

Flying Officer William "Will" Joseph Kyle (1922–1945)

Will Kyle enlisted in the Royal Canadian Air Force in September 1942. He was two years out of high school, working in an office, and engaged to be married.

Will served 449 days overseas, starting in Britain in April 1944, before being sent to India later that year. From there, he and other members of the Royal Canadian Air Force flew missions to deliver personnel and supplies to Allied ground forces in Burma.

These British and Indian forces were engaged in a series of desperate offensives in jungle terrain, facing not only the enemy, but also the hardships of monsoon rains and rampant disease.

Service file photograph of Flying Officer William Kyle.

A86 30

193712

At 11:55 a.m. on June 21, 1945, Will Kyle took off on a mission to carry supplies to Myitkina, Burma. The aircraft, a Dakota C-47, never returned.

On board with Will that day were five other members of the Royal Canadian Air Force. Their fate was unknown for decades.

Warrant Officer Class II William Bennet Rogers

Pilot William Bennet Rogers was flying the plane during the fateful mission on June 21, 1945. He had been serving in the Pacific since September 1944, completing numerous supply drops in support of ground forces.

▬ ▬

Service file photograph of Warrant Officer Class II William Rogers.

Flight Sergeant Charles Peter McLaren

Wireless operator Charles Peter McLaren was a hard worker, and his trainers saw his potential for excellence.

Service file photograph of Flight Sergeant Charles McLaren.

Leading Aircraftsman Cornelius John Kopp

Cornelius John Kopp worked as a farmer from age 16 to 24, when he enlisted in the Royal Canadian Air Force.

Service file photograph of Leading Aircraftsman Cornelius Kopp.

Warrant Officer Class I
Stanley James Cox

Stanley James Cox served
in England prior to his posting
to India in July 1944. He left
behind his new wife, Mabel,
in London.

Service file photograph of Warrant
Officer Class I Stanley Cox.

Flying Officer David "Dave" McLean Cameron

On July 7, 1945, Edna Cameron received a troubling letter. "The aircraft has been found, apparently they piled into the side of a hill," wrote a friend of her son Dave, informing her of Dave's death.

When Edna asked military officials for more information, they were baffled as to the source of this report. At that time, the six crew members were considered missing in action.

Service file photograph of Flying Officer David Cameron.

After learning of her son's disappearance, Will Kyle's mother, Edith, was advised to await further information. It was an agonizing period of anxiety and uncertainty. Although he was presumed dead in March 1946, his body was not found for decades.

In November 1990, a hunter in Myanmar (Burma) came across the wreckage of an aircraft, from which he retrieved an engraved watch belonging to Will. This discovery was brought to the attention of Veterans Affairs Canada in July 1995. Pieces of the downed aircraft were recovered.

Portion of recovered fuselage from the downed Dakota C-47.

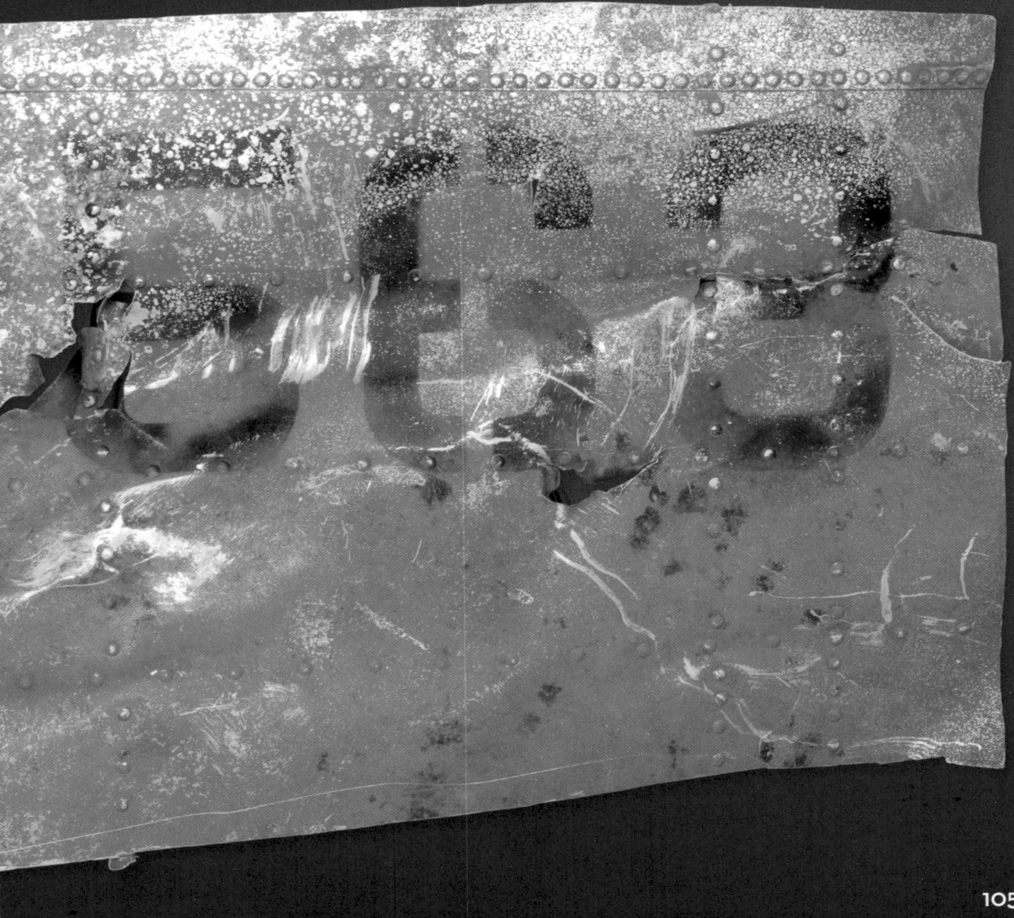

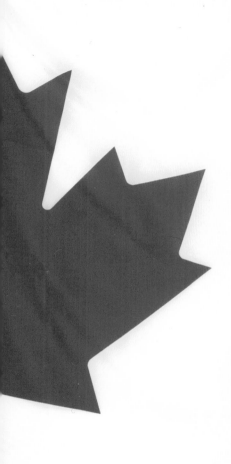

The remains of Will and the other members of the aircrew were lost in the jungle for more than 50 years. In December 1996, they were recovered.

Three months later, Veterans Affairs Canada led an official delegation of family, veterans and Canadian military personnel to Myanmar for a military funeral. This flag covered the coffin during the ceremony. All six members of the aircrew were buried together, in a single burial plot at Taukkyan War Cemetery.

A Country Shaped by War

Emerging from the ashes of war, more than one million veterans joined fellow Canadians and new arrivals to build a stronger country. Canada had been forever changed by the Second World War.

The Second World War brought Canadians together, united in the fight for victory. But it also exposed cracks in Canadian society, as the loyalty of different racial, linguistic and religious groups was called into question. Following the war, the country set out to heal these rifts, welcome new Canadians from countries still reeling from the conflict, and make room for returning veterans.

07

An unidentified Royal Canadian Air Force officer being greeted at the Ottawa, Ontario train station upon returning from Britain, September 14, 1944.

Forced Relocation

Michiko "Midge" (Ishii) Ayukawa (1930–2013)

Starting in 1941, the Canadian government stripped thousands of Japanese Canadians of their homes and businesses, and restricted where they could live.

In 1942, a racist policy forced more than 22,000 Japanese Canadians to relocate from the west coast, amid fears of a Japanese invasion. Among them were 12-year-old Michiko Ishii, her parents, and two brothers, who were moved 600 kilometres inland, to Lemon Creek, British Columbia.

It was a wrenching, demoralizing and dehumanizing experience.

After the war, Michiko adopted the anglicized name "Midge," studied chemistry and married Kaoru "Karl" Ayukawa in 1955. She started a career as a historian after a trip to Japan sparked an interest in the history of Japanese Canadian immigrants.

Michiko Ishii at Lemon Creek, British Columbia, 1945.

Starting Over

Regina (Rosenbaum) Gertner (1927–2009)

Regina (Rosenbaum) Gertner and Berek Gertner in Germany, April 1947.

Regina Rosenbaum was 16 years old when she was imprisoned in Auschwitz concentration camp. She was deemed fit for work, and transferred to Gross-Rosen concentration camp as a slave labourer. Some 40,000 people died at Gross-Rosen camp. In all, an estimated 6 million Jewish people and 5 million others were murdered in the Holocaust.

Between 1947 and 1955, around 35,000 Holocaust survivors and their dependents settled in Canada. Among the new arrivals were Regina, her husband, Berek Gertner, and their children Henry and Eric.

The Gertners found comfort and support among fellow Jewish Holocaust survivors in Toronto, Ontario.

Going for Gold

Wing Commander Hubert Brooks, M.C., C.D. (1921–1984)

On the night of April 8, 1942, during his second sortie, Hubert Brooks' aircraft caught fire over Germany. He was captured and became a prisoner of war. Hubert escaped his German captors in May 1943, and spent the rest of the war serving with the Polish resistance.

After serving his country in war, he served his country on the ice. Hubert was a member of the RCAF Flyers, a hastily assembled team of current and ex-airmen that represented Canada at the 1948 Olympic Games. The Flyers — against all odds — won Olympic gold.

Hubert retired from the military in 1971, after 31 years of service.

Hubert Brooks' RCAF Flyers
Olympic hockey jersey.

75 Years Later

Close to 1.1 million men and women
served in uniform, while 3.1 million civilians
worked in essential war industries. Almost
everyone on the home front was affected
as well. Some 45,000 gave their lives in a
necessary war against Fascism, defending
ideals in which they believed.

To mark the 75th anniversary of the end
of the Second World War, the Canadian
War Museum is proud to recognize and
honour the experiences and contributions
of those Canadians who helped advance
the Allied victory.

Second World War veterans
Nelson Langevin and Maurice Gauthier
at the Canadian War Museum, 2012.

A crowd in Ottawa celebrates
victory in Europe,
May 8, 1945.

CONTRIBUTIONS

We would like to thank the core members of the exhibition team: Stacey Barker, Arlene Doucette, Patricia Grimshaw, Jessica Shaw, Manon Tissot and the team at Haley Sharpe Design.

We also want to recognize the contributions of many colleagues at the Canadian War Museum and the Canadian Museum of History who made this exhibition possible, including Jeff Noakes, Maggie Arbour, Eric Fernberg, Meredith Maclean, Alain Simard, Shannyn Johnson, Christina Parsons, Robyne Ahmed, Erin Monette, Jennifer Potter, Kirby Sayant, Shirley Lam, Anne Macdonnell, Mona Ardestani, Ken Easton, Dave Deevey, Jean Couture, Jimmy Yousef and Ryan Dodge.

The project has benefitted from the guidance provided by Glenn Ogden, Kathryn Lyons, Peter MacLeod, James Whitham and Caroline Dromaguet.

Finally, we would like to thank Susan Ross for her outstanding photography, and Pascal Scallon-Chouinard for producing this catalogue.

PHOTO CREDITS

p. 3 © Imperial War Museum (KF 189)

p. 7 George Metcalf Archival Collection, Canadian War Museum, 20180400-002_13

p. 8 George Metcalf Archival Collection, Canadian War Museum, 20150279-001_76e

p. 11 Jack H. Smith/Canada Dept. of National Defence/Library and Archives Canada/PA-151748

p. 13 Ronny Jaques/National Film Board of Canada Photothèque/Library and Archives Canada/MIKAN no. 3197359

p. 15 Canadian War Museum, 20190178-001

p. 16 Canadian War Museum, 19750520-010

p. 17 Tilston Memorial Collection of Canadian Military Medals, Canadian War Museum, 20100138-001

p. 18 George Metcalf Archival Collection, Canadian War Museum, 20170100-001_9

p. 20 Canadian War Museum, 20030060-001

p. 21 Canadian War Museum, 19700224-029_12

p. 23 Beaverbrook Collection of War Art, Canadian War Museum, 19710261-5678

p. 25 George Metcalf Archival Collection, Canadian War Museum, 20160134-015_7b

p. 27 Beaverbrook Collection of War Art, Canadian War Museum, 19710261-4852

p. 28 Canadian War Museum, 19680136-001

p. 29 George Metcalf Archival Collection, Canadian War Museum, 20080073-005

p. 31 Tilston Memorial Collection of Canadian Military Medals, Canadian War Museum, 20080073-004

p. 33 George Metcalf Archival Collection, Canadian War Museum, 20080073-001

p. 34 George Metcalf Archival Collection, Canadian War Museum, 20180400-002_9

p. 35 George Metcalf Archival Collection, Canadian War Museum, 20180400-001a

p. 36 Canadian War Museum, 20080094-006, 001

p. 37 George Metcalf Archival Collection, Canadian War Museum, 20080094-159

p. 39 Lieut. Terry F. Rowe/Canada Dept. of National Defence/Library and Archives Canada/PA-14187

p. 41 George Metcalf Archival Collection, Canadian War Museum, 20100088-011-1

p. 42 George Metcalf Archival Collection, Canadian War Museum, 20100088-027

p. 44 Tilston Memorial Collection of Canadian Military Medals, Canadian War Museum, 20100088-002

p. 47 Lieut. Frederick G. Whitcombe/Canada. Dept. of National Defence/Library and Archives Canada/PA-163411

p. 48 George Metcalf Archival Collection, Canadian War Museum, 20170753-002

p. 49 Canadian War Museum, 20170753-001

p. 50 Beaverbrook Collection of War Art, Canadian War Museum, 19710261-2203

p. 53 Tilston Memorial Collection of Canadian Military Medals, Canadian War Museum, 20090092-001

p. 55 Lieut. Donald I. Grant/Canada Dept. of National Defence/Library and Archives Canada/PA-113659

p. 56 (background) Courtesy of Jean Brunette

p. 56 (foreground) Canadian War Museum, 20150193-001

p. 57 Canadian War Museum, 20010002-001

p. 58 Canadian War Museum, 20130345-001_2

p. 59 George Metcalf Archival Collection, Canadian War Museum, 20130345-001a

p. 60 George Metcalf Archival Collection, Canadian War Museum, 20050108-003

p. 62 George Metcalf Archival Collection, Canadian War Museum, 19830600-002_2